Some years ago, not really satisfied with the designs they had produced for the rebuilding of Stockholm's city centre, the architects in charge turned to Piet Hein. Up he came with a design, which was passed and has now become famous. This was the super-ellipse.

The white area on the front cover of this book represents Piet Hein's newly-invented shape. His super-elliptic shape mediates between the two conflicting tendencies which man has imposed upon the whole pattern of his civilisation: the one towards the rectangular, the other towards the circular.

The super-ellipse has now come to be utilised throughout the world as a solution to numerous problems within the fields of town-planning, architecture and general design. And for those who like to pretend they are fiendishly busy even in their most apathetic moments, Piet Hein has also produced the super-ellipse shape in three-dimensional form. Known simply as the 'Super-Egg'. Pocketable, useful and good fun.

MORE GROOKS

PIET HEIN

In Scandinavian countries a clever after-dinner speaker is defined as one who can talk for 30 minutes without quoting Piet Hein.

Philosopher, poet, mathematician, physicist, town planner – he has been called all these things and stands as one of the most talented of 20th century men.

'The impact of Piet Hein on the English-speaking world may be considerable. For one thing, he comes to its attention as a full-blown, developed genius with a vast number of stories, ideas and essays, poems and scientific discussions only waiting to be translated or re-expressed in English. For another thing, Piet Hein fits that currently overused description, the universal man. He stands aside the two cultures of modern life, contending they are twain only because we make them so, insisting on being artist and technologist at once and arguing convincingly that the rest of the world should too.'

Life International

PIET HEIN

MORE
GROOKS

HODDER PAPERBACKS

With the assistance of Jens Arup

© 1968 Piet Hein

First published by Borgens Forlag, Copenhagen and the Massachusetts Institute of Technology Press, Cambridge, Mass., U.S.A.

Hodder Paperback edition 1969 reproduced by arrangement with Borgens Forlag, Copenhagen.
Second Impression 1969

SBN 340 12935 2

Printed in Great Britain for Hodder Paperbacks Limited, St. Paul's House, Warwick Lane, London, E.C.4 by Hazell Watson & Viney Ltd, Aylesbury, Bucks

ATMOSPHERIC BIOGRAPHY:

by way of an Introduction

When we asked Piet Hein for some facts to constitute a short biography, his reply was to the effect that he didn't believe in facts, he believed in atmosphere—that details were for people who don't understand nuances. So we tried to put together an atmospheric biography from his many essays, and the numerous interviews and articles that have appeared throughout the world.

He started in the field of science, studying and working with things of his own at the Niels Bohr Institute in Copenhagen. But 'since science has to be misused for one of two things, the university career or technology' and he felt that he was 'more of a wild animal than a tame one', Piet Hein entered the field of invention, based on scientific knowledge, but still writing essays, fables and poems on the side.

For many years he was an acquaintance of Albert Einstein, who, intrigued by Piet Hein's mathematically based but essentially simple puzzles, spread the word to universities and from there on to the general public. Norbert Wiener, the father of Cybernetics, the science behind electronic brains, wrote his last book *God and Golem, Inc* while staying with Piet Hein in his country house in Rungsted in Denmark, and dedicated the book to him.

Recently Piet Hein was offered the post of general secretary to an international foundation which aimed to gather Nobel Laureates and other eminences from throughout the world and put them in close contact with each other. The post carried an annual salary (tax free) of 50,000 dollars. But Piet Hein remained unshaken—'I am a composer; I am not a conductor' were the words he used to get the record straight.

When the Nazis invaded Denmark in 1940, Piet Hein, at that time president of the anti-Nazi union, went underground and invented the short aphoristic poem, the grook. With its double-edged meanings and its pithy charm, the grook seemed a fine way—possibly the only way—to say the sort of humanistic and democratic things that needed to be said. He was immediately claimed 'a born classic', a descendant from the writers of the Old Nordic Havamal poems. He has written over seven thou-

sand of these to date, and has sold half a million copies of his grooks books in Denmark alone, a country with a population of less than 5 million people. Look at this in terms of the English-speaking world and you have a sale that is the equivalent of over 30 million copies.

According to Swedish and Norwegian reviews he is 'the most quoted Scandinavian', a kind of unofficial (the institution doesn't exist) Scandinavian Poet Laureate, and has often been proposed for the Nobel Prize. When Grooks finally came to be published in America they became immensely popular and were hailed in collected form as being 'a runaway bestseller' by the *New York Times*. One of the many people who reacted with great appreciation to the grooks was Charles Chaplin, with whom Piet Hein developed a close understanding.

Piet Hein regards himself as 'a characteristic specialist' because he feels he applies the same kind of creative imagination to all the types of work he tackles, thus helping to bridge the artificial chasm between the humanities and the sciences.

He interprets the enormous response to his work not as a tribute to himself so much as a highly encouraging sign that people throughout the world are wide-awake to anything that bridges the gaps in our human universe.

The Publishers.

TO
CHARLES CHAPLIN

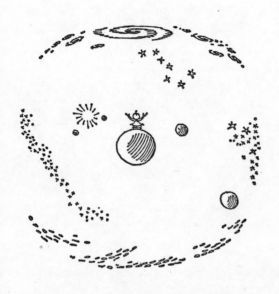

NOTHING IS INDISPENSABLE

Grook to warn the universe against megalomania

The universe may
be as great as they say.
But it wouldn't be missed
if it didn't exist.

TIME AND ETERNITY

Where the woods and ploughlands
of tradition and modernity
run into the never-ending
deserts of eternity,
there I have my daily task,
while time smoothly passes,
spooning the eternal sands
into hour-glasses.

INVESTMENT POLICY

Anxieties yield
at a negative rate,
increasing in smallness
the longer they wait.

A WORD OF ENCOURAGEMENT

Stomach-ache can be a curse;
heart-ache may be even worse;
so thank Heaven on your knees
if you've got but one of these.

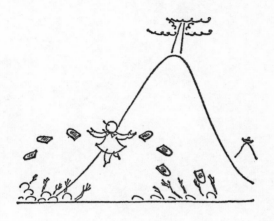

LARGESSE

A grook about giving of one's plenty

It's pleasant to give
  without feeling the price;
so let us be
  nobly profuse of
the bottomless treasure
  of moral advice
we anyhow
  never make use of.

ALLOTMENT

Your days on earth
   are just so few
that there's exactly
   time to do
the things that don't
   appeal to you.

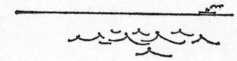

THE FINAL STEP

Motto: Il n'y a que le
dernier pas qui coûte.

If they made diving boards
        six inches shorter -
think how much sooner
        you'd be in the water.

THOUGHTS
ON A STATION PLATFORM

It ought to be plain
how little you gain
by getting excited
    and vexed.
You'll always be late
for the previous train,
and always in time
    for the next.

AN OLD SAW RESET

To keep an
ever-open door
is wisdom's true advancer;
so they are fools
who don't ask more
than ten wise men can answer.

THE UNTENABLE ARGUMENT

My adversary's argument
is not alone malevolent
    but ignorant to boot.
He hasn't even got the sense
to state his so-called evidence
    in terms I can refute.

THE WISDOM OF THE SPHERES

How instructive
            is a star!
It can teach us
            from afar
just how small
            each other are.

IT ISN'T ENOUGH

One paramount truth
our society smothers
in petty concern
with position and pelf:
It isn't enough
to exasperate others;
you've got to remember
to gladden yourself.

WHAT LOVE IS LIKE

Love is like
a pineapple,
sweet and
undefinable.

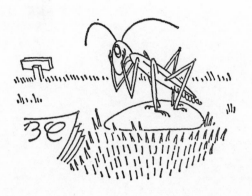

THE GRASSHOPPER'S GRIEF

A fable

A grasshopper sat on a flagstone and wept
    with a sorrow that few surpass.
He had painfully mastered his letters, and leapt
to a place where he knew an inscription was kept;
    and of course it said:
        KEEP OFF THE GRASS

SMALL THINGS AND GREAT

He that lets
the small things bind him
leaves the great
undone behind him.

BRAVE

To be brave is to behave
bravely when your heart is faint.
So you can be really brave
only when you really ain't.

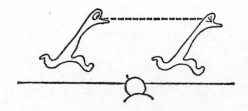

ABREAST

He who aims
to keep abreast
is for ever
second best.

ENOUGH

is more than enough

Of drink
and victuals
and suchlike
stuff
a bit
too little
is just
enough.

THE STATE

Nature, our father and mother,
gave us all we have got.
The state, our elder brother,
    swipes the lot.

POW!

That baddies are baddies
    is only too true,
however one studies
    the things that they do.
But what I find sad is
    how painfully few
have noticed that goodies
    are too.

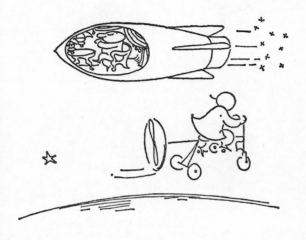

PRESENCE OF MIND

You'll conquer the present
   suspiciously fast
if you smell of the future
   —and stink of the past.

THE SLOT MACHINE

A contribution to the psychology of disappointment

> Yes, life is a gamble;
> but isn't it mean
> that you're never the one
> to win it,
> when the thing is
> a coin-in-the-slot machine,
> and you did
> put a fly-button in it.

TIMING TOAST

Grook on how to char for yourself

There's an art of knowing when.
Never try to guess.
Toast until it smokes and then
twenty seconds less.

AN ECHO FROM THE PAST

Exercise for military minds

Prehistoric monsters straying
    on a Wellsian rampage?
Martian saucerers surveying
    their terrestrial landing stage?
Say, what is that hideous braying,
    eloquent of fear and rage?
Only Homo sapiens, playing
    at the pre-atomic age.

FREEDOM

Freedom means
you're free to do
just whatever
pleases you;
- if, of course
that is to say,
what you please
is what you may.

HE ARITHMETIC OF CO-OPERATION

When you're adding up committees
there's a useful rule of thumb:
that talents make a difference,
but follies make a sum.

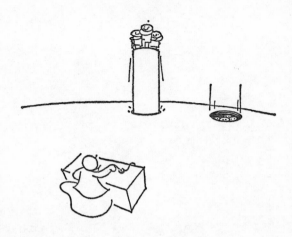

CONSTITUTIONAL POINT

Power corrupts,
whereas sound opposition
builds up our free
democratic tradition.
One thing would make
a democracy flower:
having a strong opposition -
in power.

THE OVERDOERS

Truth shall emerge from the interplay
    of attitudes freely debated.
Don't be misled by fanatics who say
    that only one truth should be stated:
truth is constructed in such a way
    that it can't be exaggerated.

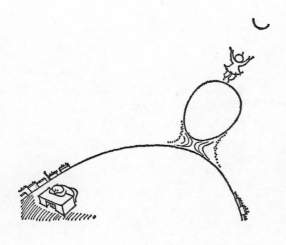

MAKING AN EFFORT

Our so-called limitations, I believe,
apply to faculties we don't apply.
We don't discover what we can't achieve
until we make an effort not to try.

RHYME AND REASON

There was an old woman
who lived in a shoe.
She had so many children.
She didn't know what to do.
But try as she would
she could never detect
which was the cause
and which the effect.

WHAT PEOPLE MAY THINK

Some people cower
    and wince and shrink,
owing to fear of
    what people may think.
There is one answer
    to worries like these:
people may think
    what the devil they please.

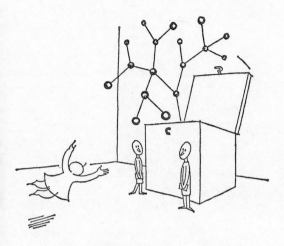

THE ONLY SOLUTION

We shall have to evolve
problem-solvers galore -
since each problem they solve
creates ten problems more.

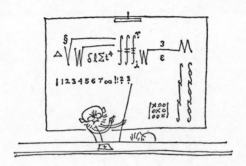

WIDE ROAD

To make a name for learning
when other roads are barred,
take something very easy
and make it very hard.

WHEN IGNORANTS-

We're leaving WISDOM
    to starve and thirst
when we cultivate
    KNOWLEDGE as such.
The very best comes
    to the very worst
WHEN IGNORANTS
    KNOW TOO MUCH.

DEAD REASONABLE

» ... that reason. died
last night at eleven.«
Henrik Ibsen: »Peer Gynt«

Somebody said
that Reason was dead.
Reason said: No,
I think not so.

REFLECTION ON SIZE

Small people often overrate
the charm of being tall;
which is, that you appreciate
the charm of being small.

A REPROOF

Grook in answer to a long explanatory letter

In view of your manner
       of spending your days
I hope you may learn,
       before ending them,
that the effort you spend
       on defending your ways
could better be spent
       on amending them.

THE FINAL TOUCH

Portrait of nobody in particular

Idiots are really
one hundred per cent
when they are also
intelligent.

THE GIOCONDA SIMILE

Certainly Leonardo's
magical Mona Lisa
may be superbly rendered
    using a dozen tiles.
Such things are not unusual.
Yet there are those who always·
feel that there's something subtle
    gone from the way she smiles

THAT'S WHY

Why do bad writers
    win the fight?
Why do good writers
    die in need?
Because the writers
    who can't write
are read by readers
    who can't read.

STONE IN SHOE

If a nasty jagged stone
gets into your shoe,
thank the Lord it came alone —
what if it were two?

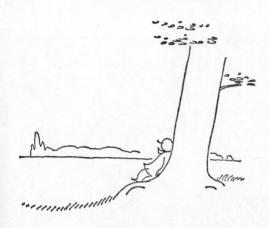

LIKE A TALL, SOLID BEECH TREE

Spring grook

I'm sitting with my back against
  a tall, solid beech tree,
feeling time flowing
  in a strong, cool stream,
feeling life rising
  like a tall, solid beech tree
emerging from Eternity's
  unending dream.

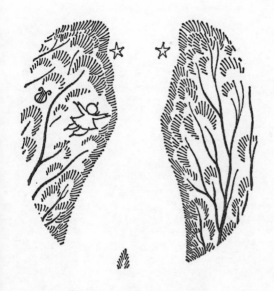

MEMENTO VIVERE

Love while you've got
love to give.
Live while you've got
life to live.

THE UNATTAINABLE IDEAL

We ought to live
each day as though
it were our last day
here below.

But if I did, alas,
I know
it would have killed me
long ago.

MEAN VALUE

We hope our share of luck will come
to some unlikely maximum.

We fear, when nightmare fears benumb,
a catastrophic minimum.

But nonetheless the final sum
is Nature's well-known middlemum.

GOOD ADVICE

Shun advice
at any price -
that's what I call
good advice.

THE ME ABOVE THE ME

Giving in is no defeat.
Passing on is no retreat.
Selves are made to rise above.
You shall live in what you love.

SUB SPECIE -

Sub specie
aeternitatis
even the dearest bought
is gratis.

WHO AM I?

Who am I
to deny
that maybe
God is me?

But how odd
If I were God.

THE ULTIMATE WISDOM

Philosophers
must ultimately find
their true perfection

in knowing all
the follies of mankind
- by introspection.

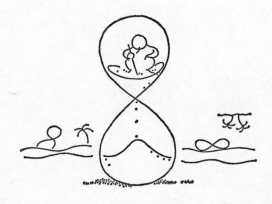

FORM AND MATERIAL

A grook about the impermanence of language

I see myself and what I write enclosed in
an hour-glass's uppermost retort.
The very stuff my patterns are composed in
must fall away, and crumble down to naught.

Yet stubbornly, and in despite of reason,
I still believe that what is fashioned there
will, when the sands run out in destined season,
remain unchanged, suspended in the air.

A TIP

to members of the literary profession

> Those
> who can write
> have a
>   lot to
> learn from those
> bright
> enough
>   not to.

ADVICE AT NIGHTFALL

Smile
a while
ere day
    is done
and all
your gall
will soon
    be gone.

TITLE INDEX

First Line Index